DEVOTIONS

CLIVE WILMER

DEVOTIONS

CARCANET NEW PRESS / MANCHESTER

Acknowledgements

Some of these poems first appeared in the following publications to whose editors thanks are due: *Aquarius, Cambridge Poetry Festival Poemcards and Posters, The Critical Quarterly, English, Infight, The London Review of Books, Pacific Quarterly, PN Review, The Poetry Review, Poetry Wales, Screever, The Southern Review, The Threepenny Review, The Times Literary Supplement* and *The Windless Orchard.* Two of the poems were broadcast on *Poetry Now* (Radio 3).

The author would like to thank The Arts Council of Great Britain for a Writer's Grant which helped him to complete this collection.

Copyright © Clive Wilmer 1982

All Rights Reserved

First published in 1982 by
CARCANET NEW PRESS LIMITED
330 Corn Exchange Buildings
Manchester M4 3BG

ISBN 0-85635-359-0

The publisher acknowledges the financial assistance of
The Arts Council of Great Britain

Printed in England by Short Run Press Ltd. Exeter

To Diane, my wife

*

Love, these are shapes of nothing, but they took
Time from our love, and time can never give
Of its own self again; so take my book,
This witness to an absence where I live.

CONTENTS

ONE
The Advent Carols / 11
Mosque / 12
Narcissus, Echo / 13
My Great-Aunt, Nearing Death / 14
To a Modern Mystic / 15
The Fall / 15
On the Demolition of the 'Kite' District / 15
After a Cremation / 16
Epitaph for a Derelict / 16
Il Palazzo Della Ragione / 17
Among Bric-A-Brac / 18
An Autumn Vision / 19
Bindweed Song / 20
Wild Flowers / 21
The Retreat / 22
Pony and Boy / 23
Beyond Recall / 24

TWO / AIR AND EARTH
Migrant / 27
Beside the Autobahn / 28
Aerial Songs / 29
Predator / 31
Natural Selection / 32
Wasteground / 34
A Victorian Cemetery / 35
On the Devil's Dyke / 37

THREE
The Natural History of the Rook / 43
Near Walsingham / 45
Home / 46
Homecoming / 47
For the Fly-leaf of a King James Bible / 49
Antiphonal Sonnets / 50

Gothic Polyphony / 51
To Nicholas Hawksmoor / 52
Venice / 53
A Woodland Scene / 54
The Parable of the Sower / 56
The Peaceable Kingdom / 58
Chinoiserie: The Porcelain Garden / 60
Prayer for my Children / 61

Notes / 63

ONE

Desire was free, and beauty's first begotten:
Beauty then neither net, nor made by art,
Words out of thoughts brought forth, and not forgotten,
The laws were inward that did rule the heart.

The Brazen Age is now when earth is worn,
Beauty grown sick, Nature corrupt and nought,
Pleasure untimely dead as soon as born,
Both words and kindness strangers to our thought.

Fulke Greville

THE ADVENT CAROLS

Aspiciens a longe

I look from afar. We stand in darkness.
A people in exile, shall we hear good news,
Who, toward midnight, in mid-winter, sing?

Sing words to call a light out of the darkness
To thaw dulled earth, to unfold her fairest bud;
Our song holds faith that the Word will be made flesh.

Now we bear candles eastward, bear them into
Inviolate dark the Word should occupy:
Light disembodied swells the sanctuary

Where an old dream is mimed, without conviction,
Over again. I look from afar. Our sung words
Are herald angels, and they announce his name,

But lay no fleshly mantle on the King,
The one Word. And yet, in the song's rising
Is rapture, and dayspring in the mind's dark:

For the one sanctuary, now, is the word not
Made flesh—though it is big with child, invaded
By the dumb world that was before it was.

MOSQUE

These arabesques on the tiles
      Will lead me nowhere;
Or to the name that is God,
      The uncomprehended.

For the aimless unnumbered perspectives
      Of column after column
We are each, at each point we move to,
      The sole focus.

Until we emerge in a courtyard
      That is open to the blue
Which a wide still pool reflects:
      Brimming over with

Call it transcendence (where noon
      With implacable glare
Effaces all), call it
      Illumination.

The dome and the minarets, blue,
      Lose themselves
In the sky, which solitary mortals
      Bow down before.

NARCISSUS, ECHO

She seeks him; but he shuns the love
Of all who are phenomenal.

Only reflection sanctifies,
For him, the beauty she holds dear.

All mass is burden; he sinks its power:
Potential drowned, the perfect flower.

He knelt to the one pure idea,
Self-love: the perfect sacrifice.

She calls and calls to him, till all
The vacant world resounds with love.

*

Only reflection sanctifies,
For him, the beauty she holds dear.
He kneels to the one pure idea,
Self-love: the perfect sacrifice.

For he has shunned all forms of love
That are, like hers, phenomenal.
She calls and calls to him, till all
The vacant world resounds with love.

*

Only reflection sanctifies,
For him, the beauty she holds dear.

She calls and calls to him, till all
The vacant world resounds with love.

MY GREAT-AUNT, NEARING DEATH

Her narrow life has straitened to this room.
Arranged like a saint's corpse in a reliquary—
Hands clasped
Over her virgin womb—
Her body lies,
Trusting that soon the hand of love will find her.
Blind eyes,
Focused on all or nothing.

Her life has known naive gentility
Only and so one thought that that defined her.
Yet charity
(Her visitors bear witness),
Though she is poor, is in her daily gift—
So call it love.

Blind hands—
Ignorant both of passion and of harm,
Hands she can barely lift—
With gentleness, conferring calm,
Reach out to where my little children stand:
They who, like her, fear nothing,
Doubt no love.

TO A MODERN MYSTIC

The Word of the beginning was your God
And in his uttering the world became.

The world grew various, beyond a name,
And god is nothing, thereby, but a word.

THE FALL

When man expelled the Lord God from the garden,
Earth yielded up its ores and fruits, till the brief
Aeons had shrivelled it; then exiled knowledge
Filled the god in him with a barren grief.

ON THE DEMOLITION OF THE 'KITE' DISTRICT

Cambridge 1980

On the smashed hearthstone or the fallen lintel
Carve words to witness:
                    That men who called themselves
Conservatives, lying in their teeth, tore down
Good rooms, good walls of weathered brick, erasing
A wordless register of birth and death.

AFTER A CREMATION

K. M. R. (1886-1978)

We laid your brother in the hallowed earth.
A ceremony and text that had served well
Four hundred years of Englishmen in death
Sufficed to bid him, graciously, farewell.

To whose shame must I set it down, that you
Were hushed and droned discreetly from the world
By some machine, to words which—though they held
No passion to beguile—said nothing true?

EPITAPH FOR A DERELICT

Here lies an oldish man whose late decay,
Early begun by drink, was held at bay
By will and great good humour: not quite sunk
In degradation; cussèd, feckless, drunk.
Now that his fellow-citizens have paid
Respects to one who lived beyond their aid,
Reader, judge only that they had been moved
Less by misfortune than the life it proved.

IL PALAZZO DELLA RAGIONE

Passing the central Palace (called 'of Reason')
In Padua, daily I'd contemplate,
High on one wall among begrimed inscriptions,

Leaning as from a window, a gentleman
In Quattrocento costume—with a turban.
He smiles across distance, his hand raised in greeting.

Smiling as if at me, to bid me welcome
To a city, enlightened and humane,
Whose style I can neither touch nor imitate.

And though I would not say,
'This is a final wisdom,
As of Christ or the Buddha, on the Palace of Reason,'

Yet it seems he has a graciousness
Beyond our time to emulate,
Though one may celebrate.

That smile across the ages is intent
On courtesy. And nonetheless,
I suffer it as though it were contempt.

AMONG BRIC-A-BRAC

The Disinherited Knight
from Scott's Ivanhoe

They do not move who ride on a glass field
That mirrors fading glory. The image cast
    Ignores the fallen shield,
The lance snapped off and the bedraggled plume.
      Among them, draped in gloom
    Rides one by his own father banished,
Yet bound in private fealty to the past,
      His armour black, unburnished.

I buy him for two pounds; toys I once held
Priceless are costly now. I had not guessed
    At what his arms withheld,
A bleakness in the loyalties which bred
      The Disinherited—
    The honour no remembered story
Could quite recover, the despair suppressed
      To flaunt a sullen glory.

AN AUTUMN VISION

In dreams, in bombed-out houses,
Where childhood used to play,
Among brambles and briar roses
And grass running to seed I pick my way,

Until I reach a clearing
Of strafed and harrowed ground
Where tombs founder, smoke blackened,
Corroded angels mourning, and no sound.

Finding the grave—a broadsword
Laid on memorial loam
As the tomb cross—and leaning forward
To gouge the sooty lichen from a name,

I glimpse beyond in the greenwood
Some purple artifice
(A helmet plume?) flourishing over
The drawn, despairing, honourable face

Of one whose quest advances
Down broken paths that tend
Towards a past locked in battle
With wrong he knows no future can amend.

BINDWEED SONG

I am convolvulus.
I prosper where your ways are undermined
By war or social lapse. So call me weed:
Bindweed that comes uncalled for, weeds that bind.

Where eyesores are I flourish—
Where mildew, rat and spider occupy
Your seat and artefact. They are the world,
You the ephemerids, and what am I

Who have wound a way back in?
—Who mesh and drape (until they all cohere)
Hedge, pathway and door-frame. See, passer-by,
How beauty decks the substance of your fear.

WILD FLOWERS

Ragwort and mallow, toadflax and willow herb
Trick out the wasteground patchwork that I thread
To no end, not for delight, but with a passion
Such as they feel who are obsessed with death—

Though this is not death. I linger here
Where rot assumes these terrace-house cadavers,
And brick-rubble, riven paving-slabs, puddled ruts
Are cordoned off by bindweed tapestries

On looms of fence-wire. One might think neglect
Cultivates that for which it has made way—
The minor glories idleness in passing
Names: 'wallflower', 'dogrose', maybe 'traveller's joy'.

THE RETREAT

for Robert Wells

There is now one perception only
comes back to him from the brilliant day
when all the bulk of the world's study

—the past's elaborate furniture
ranged in decorum, and then (mightier
still, though without substance) the future—

so weighed on him that all he could do
was run into an open meadow
and through brazen-shimmering corn—to

escape. And fling himself down just by
clear fresh water where, only less high
than trees, new grass rose into the sky.

Ah those invisible treetops! So
small he felt—as if now he could see
an innocent world again, and say

he was back where, once, all things had towered
around. In his ears, wisps of grass stirred—
that and the stream's patter all he heard

in idleness. Leant on his elbows
brinkward, but not so far as to lose
the precarious moment of his poise,

kicking his heels, he missed at the same
time the dissipation of a dream
and a child-face in the passing stream.

PONY AND BOY

    the pony presses
its muzzle into the bark
    of the tree blindly
as my boy, across the stream
leaning towards it, gazes

BEYOND RECALL

for Thom Gunn

Imprecision of the senses at midday:
stirred,
  having been struck
by the sharp bitter-sweet of a new wine
drunk in a clouded bar
     —where
to nose and tongue came the tang
of pickled onions, of briny olives and, raw
to the back of the throat, the reek
of cheap cigar smoke.

    Light
on crude gems that define a haze.
They, once possessed,—though precious
beyond recall—remain his
alone
  who inclining toward the past
hears nightingales in the dark, yet never can
transcribe
    their fluid melodies.

TWO / AIR AND EARTH

In avibus intellige studia spiritualia, in animalibus exercitia corporalia.   Richard of Saint-Victor

MIGRANT

O Redwing,
with your slashed sleeves, with
your speckled breast, the livid
stripe on your brow—

how you must stand out
against
the Iceland tundra—white
or grey—as with a
stain of your warm blood;
yet here

accommodate yourself
to songthrush and mild lawn,
and to that snow
of the new season: may,
streaking the hawthorn hedge.

BESIDE THE AUTOBAHN

It is sunk deep, this
motorway

      And all along it,
where the rats and mice—
now vulnerable, since they
cannot undermine a
causeway through their territory—
must cross,
      there perch
on fence-posts, nothing moved,
these long-eared owls
who wait

      As,
through millennia, owl
eyes have to the dusk become
enlightened:
      even so those ears,
to patterings
beneath the passing traffic, are
attuned

AERIAL SONGS

i

from his high perch
Thrush
sings the morning, from

an aerial
upon a chimney-stack—
above
the abstract foliage.

More than a
plump, warm,
speckled, dust-brown
body—he's

a voice,
awakening the city
folk
    to what
daily lost but eternal
hour of the incipient.

The tree he has alighted
on was neither
born nor dies: so he
recurs

ii

likewise, at dusk,
Blackbird his brother:
plumage
            losing
in the dark—his bright bill
sings
the sun to setting.

And the air is his!
                    For us,
            that song
articulates
the space that was
before towns were.
                    It heralds,
retrospectively,
                    the sunk
emergence of our dwellings
from the greenwood—
                    from the green
world, dark and other.

For his bill is golden,
though the wings are swart.

PREDATOR

Beneath the overarching blue,
the overarching green of
Hampstead Heath—and there we
walked, embowered in conversation

*

What should have stooped and
        flung
                down through the air
seemed, at first,
        to have
                flopped in the dust track—
some pigeon, winged
        by a stray bullet,
                toppling from the sky. Then
scuffling for a moment
        there, before
                gathering flight—
some tiny rodent struggling
        in its talons—the hawk rose.
                And as
the bat and fluttering of wings
        grew to majestic
                wingbeats the mind
saw
        what in the past
                had not been seen:

scurrying in the gutter
        the live prey; and,
                above treetop green—
soon to become
        master of earth and blood—
                poised
in the blue, the master of the air

NATURAL SELECTION

At first sight, *house-martins*
I thought: for what
other bird, what passerine, would lodge
so?—then I saw
the sparrow, peering from
no nest but a dark cavity
beneath the eaves.
          Splendid more
than is commonly acknowledged:
this one, male—with his
grey crown and black bib, not so
mousy as the female—pert
scavenger: always
I've admired them
who, of all winged things, are fittest
to adapt.
      The house-martins and
all the swallow-kind, who with grace arch
our thoroughfares, have blessed
time out of mind—with
is it trust?—our home walls where they
build their nests: a natural
benediction.
        But the sparrows, not
the offspring of a freehold
freely entered into, now breed
in a mousehole, thrive
on dereliction.

     *

     It is our
improvidence that has made way
for a world fit for what
nature (we say) *selects*; and we,

when we speak so, become
the self-elect, standing outside
the world we must now leave
to the once-welcome sparrow
and the rat—to cranny-dwellers, all
whose empires (our bequest
unwilled) shall flourish
where we die.
          And a dead world
we shall leave—crumbling
brickwork, rotting
eaves and rafters, songless
wood: a world stripped
of its old glories, where every
edifice of man
or god is gutted and
laid waste.
          The eagles
are departing now; not us,
still less the martins, we
shall not be the survivors.

WASTEGROUND

this vacant lot
            that's
puddled rutted patched with litter
a short cut   a blank space
between work and home
(day after day)
this dreary season

cast upon my outward
eye my dull year's first
bright goldfinches
two fists
            unclenched
flung red and yellow
on the unredeemed
      vacancy
            of the air

A VICTORIAN CEMETERY

Peace, perfect peace.

He giveth His Beloved sleep.

Such pious apophthegms
preface the tensed calm
of the cemetery I walk through
every Sunday, which today
seems attuned to my
blurred autumnal mood:
a melancholy
             a light mist
burnished with bronze and gold.

And rooks
rise and settle
on larch, elm, yew; or wheel
slowly about, haunting
the air beyond this place,
the tips of those great wings
etching upon the sky
the unseen compass of
a territory:

           which is their right
and proper realm—a
nether-world of quiet
despond
        held down
and only through
the forlorn hopes inscribed
on monuments, now
tottering, made articulate.

To this grove the spirits
of the Age's gentlefolk,

borne here perhaps
on the rook's wing, withdrew
for sleep, for peace.

ON THE DEVIL'S DYKE

for Michael Vince

In the hedgerows
           along this walk
songbird nests abound; and—
           as my dog runs on
interpreting
           on air and earth
rank traces and warm lingerings that
her cold nose pursues
           ahead of me—
the birds flutter out and away;
and beasts of undergrowth and hedgerow,
           rabbit fox and weasel,
stir within the radius of her scenting
unseen mostly,
           though from time
to time
           ahead of us
a red or brown
           streaks
the crisp white of the chalk ridge, and passes
through the eye's enduring field
           of green
and brown-and-green
           bound
in the clasp of the arched blue.
           There the skylarks
our footfalls drive from the warm clench of
nestling in the grass
           appear and disappear,
become what is the
           audible extent
—beyond sight—
           of the sky.

      *

One might as well
            be walking further south,
the chalk hills there, it could be
            the South Downs.
But no:
            this is a made place, here
in the deep bone and sanctum
            of the land
is stamped the signature,
            the *homo fecit*,
of those who dug what we
            still call,
as the feared Norsemen did,
            a *dyke*—
no Saxon *ditch* (where a tramp
            might bed down).

            *

Defence
            was what they had in mind
who with this causeway
            bridged the fen to guard
their one landward flank—so
            to insulate a territory
plants birds and beasts
            ignore. And though you pass
from time to time
            into some tangled hedge,
are drawn into
            —enmeshed in, even—
green of the earth's making,
            yet you emerge
out on the bare ridge-way
            and, across the trench,
survey
            the furrowed ploughland in retreat,

envisage
        the advance of bristling armies
held
        in your long watch.

    *

A spring day
        and I lie back
on the full flank of the earth,
        the sloped wall of the bulwark.
I am weight, borne by what
        holds me down—
as the larks
        rise, till they are
out of range and
        the blank sky is all
the eye beholds,
        the heart and ear
tugged
        by a lilt and stagger that ascend
beyond perceiving: air,
        their scope of territory, their
earthly dwelling.

        Listen!
sing the larks
        down to me: *you,*
a man, live in a place. More,
        in a palimpsest of places:
landscape history creed the word.
Through us you may infer those
        other worlds your map
and composite of places must at best
imply.
        Worlds often glimpsed
beyond your earthworks, ramparts, palisades.

                              (East Anglia)

THREE

If I called God a being it would be just as wrong as to call the sun pale or black. God is neither this nor that.

Meister Eckhart

THE NATURAL HISTORY OF THE ROOK

The rooks are Gothick which have brought to mind
The naturalist Charles Waterton. He wrote
With care and indignation: an explorer:
A solitary who loved, above all creatures,
The birds of the air. When at his burial
A linnet sang out, fact gave rise to legend:
That the flotilla of black barges floating
His body to its lakeside grave had been
Escorted by long flights of birds in mourning.

Among them, rooks. From trees they pinnacle
Like symptoms of a fantasy, their humped
Black shapes unfold now, lifting, taking wing
To drape the sky with signs of lamentation.

No. Waterton—who one phantasmal night
Of gloom and tempest wrote in quietness,
Not fantasy not legend, but 'the history
Of the rook'—in the rook saw no gloom, would not
Submit to the 'blue devils' conjured up
By the November fogs but would combat them
With 'weapons of ornithology'.

                He had—
'Having suffered himself and learned mercy'—
Laid his guns down, walled in his park and lake,
And made a pause in nature. There he watched,
Rejoicing in cacophony—explored
Downward
            toward a silence
                   undisturbed
The barn-owl winged its day through,
                      made a space
Where rooks alighted, their gregarious croak
In tune with an unheard polyphony

His prose, which does not venture to transcribe it,
Bespeaks. Of science and his own estate
He made himself
                 a sanctuary
                         the mind
Questing could enter into, haunt in freedom,
And dwell in, freed of its own hauntings.

                                            Blithe
You must have been, Charles Waterton, to know
That the inequitable penal laws
Enforced by ignorance and sentiment
Against all 'pests and vermin', now repealed
By you, no longer warped the needful cycles
Of breeding and predation. Blithe you were
From your high perch to watch the darting turquoise
Spear the still pool, to hear the barn-owl screech
No special doom to man, and see the rooks
Fly overhead in the dawn light to pass
Into the still-remote, unmediated
Variety of inhuman atmosphere.

NEAR WALSINGHAM

Springs rise where saints have prayed,
    Tradition says;
  And tells of rivulets and wells
    Conceived of rumoured deities.

But streams would have obeyed
    No peremptory hand.
  Where water has already blessed the land
    Saints choose to pray.

Gods walk when glint and spade
    Strike, as it brims,
  A buried watercourse. And one dreams
    A cryptic meaning for the source:

Meaning which haunts the shade
    That falls by bridge and ford,
  Lodged in the thought and speech that hearken toward
    The interminable

Tale given and not made
    Or understood,
  Which haunts the place. What we might say
    Of what it tells would speak of God.

HOME

after Cesare Pavese

The lone man hearkens to the calm voice,
His expression ajar—as if the draught
On his face were a breath, a friendly breath,
Returning, beyond belief, from time gone by.

The lone man hearkens to the ancient voice
His fathers throughout the ages have heard, clear
And composed, a voice that much like the green
Of the pools and hills deepens at evening.

The lone man knows a voice of shadow,
Caressing, and welling forth in the calm tones
Of a secret spring: intently his eyes closed
He drinks it down, and seems not to have it near him.

It is the voice that, one day, halted the father
Of his father, and each of the dead blood.
A woman's voice that whispers in secret
On the threshold of home, at the fall of darkness.

HOMECOMING

A Theme and Variations

1. Mid-winter

The year goes out in wrath. And through the winter
Are scattered little days like cottages.
And lampless, hourless nights; and grey mornings,
Their indistinguishable images.

Summertime, autumn—time and season passing,
And brown death has seized on every fruit.
And new cold stars appear now in the darkness,
Unseen before, even from the ship's roof.

Pathless is every life. And every path
Bewildered. The end unknown. And whoso seeks
And finds a path finds that his utterance breaks
Off in sight of it, empty the hands he shakes.

2. A Winter Evening

When snow falls on pane and sill,
Long peals are borne on evening air;
The board is laid for many there
In a house provided well.

On their wanderings, several others
Come to the gate by dark ways.
Gold blossoms the tree of grace
Where cool sap in the earth gathers.

The wanderer quietly steps across
A threshold pain has turned to stone.
On the board glow bread and wine
In all the radiance of loss.

3. A Threshold

You, centaury, o lesser star,
You birch, you fern, you oak:
Near me you stay as I go far . . .
Home, into your snare we walk.

Black on a bearded palm tree
Hangs cherry-laurel bunched like grapes.
I love, I hope, I believe . . .
The small date, split open, gapes.

A saying speaks—to whom? To itself: *Servir*
Dieu est régner . . . I can
Read it, I can—it is coming clear—
Get out of Me-no-unnerstan.

after Georg Heym, 'Mitte des Winters'
Georg Trakl, 'Ein Winterabend'
Paul Celan, 'Kermorvan'

FOR THE FLY-LEAF OF A KING JAMES BIBLE

'. . .in dürftiger Zeit'
—Hölderlin

Now, in our needy time,
These words so flush with hope
Probe at the heart that aches toward the past
For the god not yet come.

Cadence and phrase and tone—
Derived by Jacobean
Divines from Tyndal and from Coverdale,
Refined—gain resonance.

A rhythm draws the mind
Through theirs to older scores:
Lollard and Saxon drafts; Latin behind,
A plainchant barely heard.

Then Greek, Hebrew, the first
Utterance of the word
Of one the many tongues have, differently,
Called 'God' with the same thirst.

This text—new from the press—
Already smelt of a time
Past, as if left to fust in cellars: earth-
begrimed, already foxed.

Now, in our needy time,
Virtue and beauty seem
In dark, like heady vintage, to mature:
Full-bodied and obscure.

ANTIPHONAL SONNETS

Of John Taverner

1.

Suppose a man were dying and this sound
Washed over him: it would be like, not sleep,
Not dream, but setting eyes for the first time
On the world, ours, yet other. For the sense
Of things would be the things themselves and words
Would gem the melismatic harmony
Rarely, articulating it. The mind—
In a language, the great mass of whose words
Are shattered into vagrant syllables
By gay polyphony—would edge towards
The scope of revelation, which is speechless.
Now, in the place of death, an angel sits
And speaks to three who mourn of interim,
Announces that the second day is done.

2.

This was the world: the word.
                                        Gratuitous day,
Stained by a red or a blue glaze, confined
By aspiring stone to space with no horizon:
Earthly things that composed an allegory
Which guessed at heaven. He cast given speech
Against the bossed and starry vaults, shattered it
To falling fragments, harmonies—a fertile
Resonance, as much like beauty as like that
It seemed at length to mask: in empty space
A simple disembodied word, the truth.
Then beauty was the hoofbeats in the nave,
The radiant shower of glass, a mace that knocked
Devotion from her pedestal, the flames
That burnt the rood in the broad light of day.

GOTHIC POLYPHONY

Space: tall, with no horizon. Plainsong scales
And vines the branched and foliating thrust
Of stone: to bloom polyphony: which fails
Against the ribbed vault's bossed and fretted crust.

TO NICHOLAS HAWKSMOOR

When, as at Beverley Minster or All Souls,
You ape the Gothic, art is all facade.
Forms moulded of your substance, clear and hard,
Weigh with a Roman virtue. What controls

The impulse, at Christ Church, that would have soared
Through broken cornices to where a spire
Defined not form but anguish and desire,
Becomes your very theme at Castle Howard,

The Mausoleum. Private grief, though lost
In generalities of hope resigned,
There haunts the orders which the patient earth

Sustains for ruin. And something of the north
Troubles your cool sobriety of line
With aspiration and an edge of frost.

VENICE

Salt-bleached marble, the green stain of seaweed.

A face the sea dismembers and remembers
Looks back at those who lean towards it, drowning
In admiration, in reflected glory.

Here man hath set his footprint on the waters.
We see the tides disperse it, see them relinquish
The white of marble and the green of seaweed.

A WOODLAND SCENE

We think we detect a date: in the 1860's is it?—for that would fit. But no, it is merely a calligraphy of shadow and reflection, which leaves (overhanging it) have trailed across the stream in the foreground.

Then the painter's name, Maltby. This, we find, occurs in the standard reference book, but with different initials.

*

Watercolour, overlaid with bodycolour. 'Ruskinian,' a friend calls it. And so it is: in its anxious piety—in the endeavour to speak, crisply, of the transitory variegations of light on bark or, where a bough has been shorn off, of light on pith; everywhere modified by the intervention of leaves, translucent or shadow-casting. Ruskinian, too, in the implied continuity of the given world with whatever a mesh of boughs and branches, contained within an arbitrary rectangle, can itself contain. Speaking, then, of the world at large, the picture expounds no painter, is devotional.

Encrusted with light, the leaves lose substance. Fretted with bodycolour, surface becomes depth. It is a sunny day. In our looking, we cool ourselves on the banks of a stream. We are somewhere in the depths of a wood. No people, no birds or beasts, and the world is still.

*

The craftsman who will restore it seems to care as much for frame, mount and glass as for the picture. 'Fine hand-made glass, that,' and how can he tell? He holds it horizontal to the eye and, see, light moves in waves across the lucid, tumbling surface, as if engendered by the glass itself. A still, translucent sea—becalmed—of greens and blues. Hung in its frame the glass, like the foliage it reserves for us, both absorbs and reflects, draws in and throws back such light as has entered the room. To the eye of the room-dweller, it interprets the light of the forest.

The frame is of oak. Dull with bituminous varnish and begrimed, until I stripped it with caustic. Then as the water dried, a rose-colour seemed to flush, elusively, in the damp grain of it. We shall preserve what we can of that, and the glass. But the mount has decayed, gone brown; and the card the picture was stuck on is pocked with mould—'Foxing,' says the craftsman: an impurity in the glue can cause it, or a dead fly. All this must be renewed.

*

It used to hang, I remember, in the dullest room of my parents' house, a room usually locked. Later, I rescued it from a windowless boxroom. I have hung it near a window now, well in the light.

On occasion, the shade of the room blends with the shade of the woodland. Though often, where a treetrunk casts its shadow, daylight falls. Or the pool of imperfect glass becomes opaque with reflections that ripple above inferred profundity. From the other side of the room one begins to see (after long acquaintance) how the picture's uniformity of surface actually appears to tilt inwards, receding into distance through a region of paint where the light's greenish tints are touched with blue.

*

This blue is a threshold, the frame its gate or door. The wood is uninhabited. Let the picture's making and preserving restore to the woodland its absent spirits, recall to the hearthside our household gods.

THE PARABLE OF THE SOWER

*Stained glass in the Arts & Crafts style,
set in a medieval church*

I

The sower goes out to sow. His sense and form
Move only in a landscape of stained glass;
    The leads like ivy stems,
    Enmeshing, bind him in.
Outside, it is afternoon; inside, the sun
Irradiates a face in shadow—eyes
    Inclined toward the earth
    Crimsoning underfoot.
The glory round about and through his limbs
Is vision in excess of daily need,
    Devotion in the work
    Dispersed beyond the seed.

II

Victorian glass of eighteen ninety-seven,
Replacing the clear light in the west wall
    In homage to a time
    That built as if for ever.
The vision is of a vision that transfigured
Perspectives on the bare field; but with skill
    The craftsman has contained,
    Edged, the unearthly glow.
His observation accurate, the self
A blemish that his labour should efface,
    Devotion to his craft
    Speaks through the pictured face.

III

The sower does not see the field he sows.
He walks in rapture, but his eyes are vague
      With sorrow not his own,
      That has no root in earth.
It is the craftsman's sorrow, for he gave
These paradisal colours to the earth
      But when he looked on earth
      He found an absence there.
Here wayside, thorn, good ground and stony ground
Are stained through with devotion, with his need
      For things to mean—the word
      Secreted in the seed.

THE PEACEABLE KINGDOM

for Tamsin and Gabriel

*The wolf also shall dwell with the lamb, and the leopard
shall lie down with the kid; and the calf and the young lion
and the fatling together; and a little child shall lead them.*

This morning, as I watch my son
    Play with a loved toy horse so small
    He need not fear it, I recall
His elder sister, not yet one,

Behind her cot-bars, turning to peep
    At me or, through the orbit of
    The animals that wheeled above
Her head, to watch enlarging sleep

Involve her tiny world—her laugh
    Hushed, and her babble, that addressed
    And answered it. Like things possessed,
Kangaroo, tiger and giraffe,

Pivoted from an elephant's
    Huge bulk, in genial caricature
    Grinning in disregard of her,
Went by her with a nod or prance.

Animals prowling through the air
    In cycles of pursuit, restrained
    From conflict by the space ordained
For harmony of movement: where

Else could the like be found but in
    A mind whose thoughts cannot efface
    With reasoning that longed-for place,
The garden of our origin?

—Which she had glimpsed, who thought and saw
    Nothing she could have known, a child
    Looking with trust upon the wild
Through distance unaccounted for.

Could this be that Arcadia,
    Where 'inward laws that ruled the heart'
    Ruled nature, the Creator's art,
As well? Man the Artificer

Then was not: for his work presents,
    Apart from us, a world we stand
    Apart in and would understand;
He frees it from inconsequence,

Showing us—through attention paid
    To things the distances remove—
    That what is feared with reason, love
Need not renounce. Therefore he made

That mobile bestiary whose course
    My girl watched, and these animals
    Cluttered inside their farmyard walls,
Now, by my boy, who lifts a horse

As if he thought to elevate
    The mystery of flesh and blood,
    Priest-like, toward an unknown god,
To praise, and to propitiate.

CHINOISERIE: THE PORCELAIN GARDEN

Empty, flicked by a fingernail, the bowl
   Rings with the charm of vacancy. A girth
Of pure abstraction binds your world: a whole,
Void of anxiety and fond recall,
                That stands free of the earth.

Revellers in blue glaze, your endless day
   Persuades you there is ground for careless mirth
That does not cloy. Nothing you do or say
Has death in it, as if your primal clay
                Were not derived from earth.

The matter of your converse? Nothing said.
   What profits you, what is your life there worth?
You smile. (Olympian . . . Mandarin . . .) The dead,
Even, could not be more disinterested
                Or less ruled by the earth.

On the calm surface of the pool appears,
   Stood on its head, the world that gave you birth,
Denied you growth. And our world is to yours
What you are to the pool, whose rippling clears
                Inconsequence from earth.

There you look on, and we glimpse paradise:
   A dream of beauty and a form of dearth.
One touch of pain, unmimed, might turn to vice
Your virtues. Beauty is gloss. Like constant ice,
                Polar, yet of the earth.

PRAYER FOR MY CHILDREN

Te lucis ante terminum

Before the end of daylight, Lord
    Dweller in things, we pray you keep
    The custom of your watch when sleep
Annihilates you in our thought.

Untrouble us with dreams; the grim
    Phantasmagoria of the night
    Remove. In sleep the inward sight
Wakes and is powerless to condemn.

And, distant Father, if you hear
    The outcry of a sleeping child,
    Keep soul and body undefiled.
Then, in the absence, you are near.

NOTES

'On the Demolition of the "Kite" District', p. 15. The Kite is a modest residential district of central Cambridge which has suffered from planning blight for a number of years. Much of it was finally demolished in the spring of 1980.

'On the Devil's Dyke', p. 37. The dyke is a large earthwork, about 7½ miles in length, near the Cambridgeshire-Suffolk border. It is thought to have been built to defend the kingdom of East Anglia against incursions along the Icknield Way.

'The Natural History of the Rook', p. 43, includes quotations from Charles Waterton's *Essays on Natural History*. Waterton (1782-1865) turned his estate at Walton Hall, Yorkshire, into the world's first wild-life sanctuary.

'Antiphonal Sonnets', p. 50, deal with the life of the polyphonic composer John Taverner (c. 1495-1545), who renounced all musical activity shortly after his conversion to Protestantism. He was employed by Thomas Cromwell in the spoliation of the monasteries. The first sonnet alludes to his Respond, 'Dum transisset sabbatum', a setting of *St Mark* xvi, 1-2; the second to a letter from Taverner to Cromwell—'according to your lordship's commandment the Rood was burned the seventh day'.

'To Nicholas Hawksmoor', p. 52. All Souls is the Oxford College, but Christ Church is the parish church of Spitalfields in the East End of London.

'Prayer for my Children', p. 61, is loosely based on the sixth-century hymn, 'Te lucis ante terminum'. (See *The Penguin Book of Latin Verse*, p. 113.)